Noko the Knight

Empowering Kids to Embrace Their Emotions Effectively

By Eleni Theodorou

Illustrated By Aaron Laroc

NATURE'S NIGHT SCHOOL

Noko the Knight: Empowering Kids to Embrace Their Emotions Effectively

Copyright © 2015 Eleni Theodorou

Illustrated by Aaron Laroc

Printed in the United States of America

Summary: When Noko finds out he is soon to become a big brother, he is overcome by a mix of emotions, not realizing how his behavior affects those closest to him.

BISAC: JUV013040:
JUVENILE FICTION / Family / New Baby

Library of Congress Cataloging-in-Publication Data
Theodorou, Eleni
Noko the Knight: Empowering Kids to Embrace Their Emotions Effectively
First Edition
ISBN Paperback: 978-0-9962719-0-5
ISBN ebook: 978-0-9962719-1-2
1. Children's animal book 2. African kids' tale 3. Early social skills 4. Children's adventure
5. New baby story
Library Of Congress Control Number: 2015908020

Disclaimer

Author's Dedication

It is with my whole heart that I dedicate this book to my wonderful, loving parents and sister who have been incredibly supportive of me, consistently spurring me on to explore the soulful path I have always been destined to pursue. Baba, Mom and Margz, I love you ~ THANK YOU.

I also dedicate this book to our other Sunshine Child, my Godson Ariano. Ari, I love and adore you to the moon and beyond and I look forward to sharing many more mischievous adventures together!

Author's Acknowledgements

My appreciation and sincere thanks go to each and every dear family member and friend who has supported me, believed in me, and guided me ~ I send much love and light to each of you.

Furthermore, I wish to express my deepest gratitude to our wonderfully gifted illustrator, Aaron Laroc. It has been a pleasure working with you Aaron ~ your enthusiasm, dedication and professionalism is truly admired and appreciated. Thank you so very much for bringing Noko and his friends to life!

Arnaldo Nunez is one more friend, a talented graphic designer whom I wish to sincerely thank. Arnaldo, your patience, guidance and assistance with the logo, web design, and book layout (in three languages!) is very appreciated!

Eva Fattahi, it has been a wonderful working with you in developing the marketing and PR side of "Noko the Knight". This learning curve is invaluable to me. Thank you so much for your friendship and dedication in helping me bring Noko and his friends to the world.

Introduction

Noko the Knight is the first African tale of a series, written from the heart with the aim of enhancing communication and strengthening the bond between Parent and Child. There are a variety of activities at the end of the story, which are geared toward opening dialogue between reader and listener, giving the caregiver an opportunity to positively shape a child's emotional well-being.

Readers will learn about the beauty of South Africa, as this tale is geographically and ecologically accurate, with vibrant illustrations to match. With the inclusion of a variety of nocturnal creatures, the appreciation of diversity is also highlighted, thereby encouraging a deeper understanding of those around us who are different, in a compassionate setting.

Where do Noko and his friends live in South Africa?

Africa

Limpopo Province

North West

Gauteng Mpumalanga

Free State

KwaZulu-Natal

Lesotho

Northern Cape

Eastern Cape

Western Cape

South Africa

Bushveld:

A subtropical woodland region in South Africa, made up of well-grassed plains that are dotted by dense clusters of trees and tall shrubs.

Ahhh Mama Afrika... How you bless us with your warm, summer sunsets that linger with the sweet scents of the Mpumalanga bushveld.

It is at the end of this hot African day that all the creatures of the night come out to play! One of these curious creatures is little Noko - a young crested porcupine with a big heart and even bigger dreams.

As soon as the sun started to disappear behind the beautiful Drakensberg Mountains, Noko scurried out of the family burrow to go meet up with his friends at Nature's Night School - Mmabudu the aardwolf, Kolobe the warthog, Nkwe the leopard cub and Inyoka the young African rock python - all of whom are always happy to see him!

Suddenly, Noko was called back into their family burrow by his parents, Mr. and Mrs. Porcupine, who were eagerly waiting to tell him some exciting news...

Noko dropped his furry little head and reluctantly turned around, wandering lazily back home.

Upon his entrance into the burrow, Mr. and Mrs. Porcupine stood side by side, brimming with pride as Mr. Porcupine gleefully announced that Noko was soon to become a big brother!

Noko, who for so long was the only baby in the family, stood in front of his thrilled parents in shock. "Big brother? What do you mean I am going to be a big brother? I am the baby of this family and it's going to stay that way!" he cried out.

Before his prickly parents could say another word, Noko spun around on his little paws and dashed out of the burrow into the darkness of the bushveld.

Whilst meandering around restlessly in the darkness of the night, Noko was overcome by a mix of emotions; a little sad, a little unsure, and even a little jealous. "How could this be?" he grumbled to himself in disbelief.

"Now I am not going to be able to spend much time with Mommy and Daddy after school playing in the forest together. By playing together, Daddy teaches me valuable skills I need as a growing boy such as foraging for roots and other treats from the forest and farmland.

Now he is going to be too busy with the new baby porcupine and not have any time for me. AND, I am going to have to share my room in the burrow with the baby!" he said out aloud to himself.

Unbeknownst to him, his friend Inyoka the
African rock python was slithering near to where
Noko was and had overheard what Noko was
saying.

"What'sss the matter dear Noko?" Inyoka lisped
inquisitively as he sailed around Noko. At first
Noko was startled by Inyoka as he thought he
was alone.

Then, without warning, Noko's little quills rose quickly into the shape of a crest, making him look even bigger and scarier as he bellowed out, "What are you doing here, Inyoka? Why are you listening in on me?!"

Before Inyoka could reply, Noko started to shake with anger and his quills started to rattle, making a loud noise, which seemed to be a warning, truly frightening Inyoka.

As his friend, Inyoka was trying to understand what was bothering Noko so much but before he could ask him another question, Noko's quills started shooting out at him.

"Ow! Ow! Ow!" Inyoka exclaimed as Noko's quills pierced his scaly skin. "Why are you hurting me Noko? I am your friend!" Inyoka cried out. As the quills continued shooting in his direction, Inyoka had no option but to quickly retreat to get far away from the sharp pain.

Back at Nature's Night School, Mmabudu the aardwolf, Kolobe the warthog and Nkwe the leopard cub were all waiting impatiently for Inyoka and Noko to arrive so that they could start their evening class.

"I wonder what's keeping our two buddies? Class is about to begin!" grunted Kolobe. Just as she finished her sentence, in slithered Inyoka, looking sad, tired and very uncomfortable.

"Where have you been?" inquired the group in unison. With his eyes cast down, Inyoka told them that he had come across Noko in the forest on his way to school and that the porcupine seemed very unhappy.

Inyoka continued to explain to his friends, "When I tried to understand what was bothering him, he rattled with anger and some of his quills shot out at me, impaling my skin and it hurts!" Inyoka turned around to show them the sharp quills in his side.

Kolobe, Nkwe and Mmabudu were stunned. "That doesn't sound like Noko," said Nkwe in disbelief. "Something must really be bothering him for this to happen because he has such a kind heart and truly cares for his friends," he proceeded as Mmabudu gently tried to remove the quills from Inyoka's side.

Back in the woods, Noko was still roaming around thinking about the news he'd just been given when he suddenly realized that he actually had to be at school, and was late!

He quickly shook off the dust and leaves his little quills had picked up when they were sharply raised earlier on and scurried through the bushveld to get to class.

Upon arrival at school, all of his friends were waiting for him in the courtyard bearing concerned, yet puzzled looks on their faces.

Shy Mmabudu plucked up his courage and bravely stepped forward as Noko approached them. When Noko saw Mmabudu step forward he realized something was amiss as Mmabudu rarely took the lead in their group.

Noko also saw his friend Inyoka curled up in pain behind his other friends and realized that Mmabudu was about to address his poor behavior towards the snake. Noko slowly lowered his head in shame, unable to look his friend in the eye.

"Noko," Mmabudu started, "you are our friend and we all love you very much. This is why I come to you, to try to understand what happened in the forest with you and Inyoka."

Noko took a deep breath and began to explain to his friend that he had just heard that his parents were about to have another baby porcupine and that this really shocked him. This also let him feel all sorts of emotions, all of which Noko was trying to make sense of while he was in the forest.

Noko apologetically continued, "I thought I was alone in the forest when suddenly Inyoka was behind me and startled me with his curious question. I was not expecting anyone to be near me, let alone hear my uttered frustrations and before I knew it, my quills rose quickly and I couldn't stop myself from shaking.

I know Inyoka meant well, but I was so caught up with these mixed feelings within me that shortly after my quills rose, I struggled to keep them from shooting out at anyone close to me.

I truly did not mean for my friend to get hurt" Noko confessed, with big, glossy tears welling up in his little eyes.

Mmabudu sensed that Noko was being sincere and turned to look at his friends behind him, beckoning them to come forward, including Inyoka.

One by one each of his friends came closer to Noko until they all surrounded him, reaching out their little paws. Inyoka also came forward and wrapped his prickled tail around them all, embracing Noko with a loving group hug.

"Noko," Nkwe purred, "thank you for sharing your feelings with us as we didn't understand why you had lashed out at our friend Inyoka with your sharp quills.

We know you have a good heart and that you wouldn't ever do anything to hurt anyone intentionally."

Noko managed to lift his furry head to look at each of his friends and said, "Thank you for being patient with me. It means so much to me that you tried to understand me better first instead of scolding me or even ignoring me.

You truly are dear friends indeed and I appreciate you all so much."

A few sunrises and sunsets passed and Noko was feeling more settled with the expectation of his new sibling.

Mama and Papa Porcupine spent extra time with him, explaining that as a big brother, he would have a very important role in helping his parents take care of their new baby and that he would always be deeply loved, and is very special to them.

Not long afterwards, Noko and his friends had just finished class at Nature's Night School and were playing in the dusty courtyard when in burst another dear friend of theirs, Tiny Tarentaal, out of breath and with her spotted feathers all ruffled.

"Noko!" she sputtered. "Quick! Quick! Quick! You have to hurry back to the burrow as your family needs you now!" Noko was ever so puzzled yet trusted Tiny Tarentaal and dashed off into the forest as fast as his little legs could carry him, forgetting to say goodbye to the others.

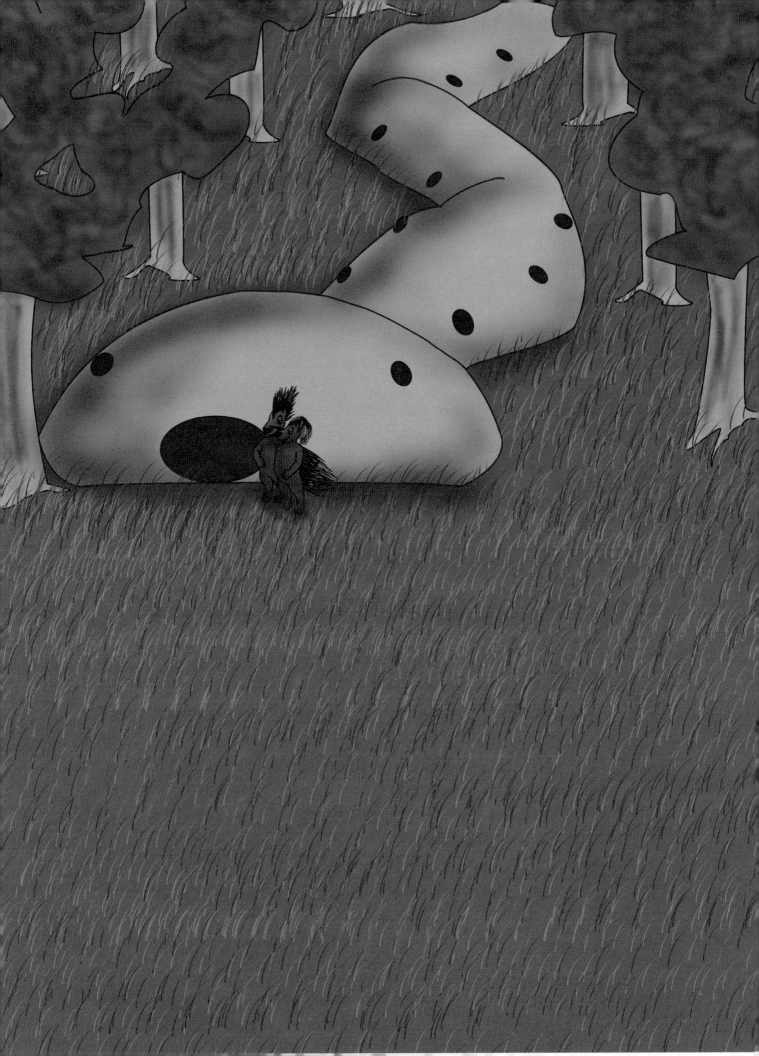

Back at the burrow, Mr. and Mrs. Porcupine were waiting anxiously for their young son to come home from school as, while Noko was away, his proud parents had unexpectedly welcomed their little baby girl into the world!

A few short moments later, in rushed Noko through the burrow entrance. He was pleasantly surprised by the smiles of his parents, along with the gurgling sounds of his new baby sister!

"Wow…" Noko thought to himself, "she looks so small and sweet, ever so precious". Before he could say anything, Mr. Porcupine came up to Noko and put his proud paw on his son's shoulder.

"Son, you are our baby girl's big brother now and she is going to need her wise brother to help teach her those skills we learned in the woods together. Are you up for this adventure?" Without hesitation, Noko squealed with delight. "Absolutely, Dad! This is my duty!"

And with this, Noko scampered over to his sister's crib and whispered into her ear, "Welcome, little Lady! I am Noko, your big brother, and I will make sure you grow up strong like me. I will protect you here in the Mpumalanga bushveld."

Baobab tree:

This is one of the grandest and toughest trees with two of it's species native to Africa. These trees can reach up to 98 feet (30 metres) in height and its trunk circumference up to 154 feet (47 metres)! This majestic tree can also hold up to 26,000 gallons (100,000 litres) of water in it's trunk to endure the harshest of droughts.

As a core part of our story, the baobab tree is also representative of the strength of the family and the community at large as it offers shelter, support, nourishment and life to all, even through the toughest times.

Did you know that Noko and his friends have true African tribal names?
Let's pronounce and write our little friends' names together!

Noko
NÓ-ko
N ___ ___ ___
Noko means porcupine in Tswana

Inyoka
In-yÓ-ka
I ___ ___ ___ ___ ___
Inyoka means snake in Zulu

Mmabudu
Mma-bÙ-du
M ___ ___ ___ ___ ___ ___
Mmabudu means aardwolf in Tswana

Kolobe
Ko-lÓ-be
K ___ ___ ___ ___ ___
Kolobe means warthog in Sotho

Nkwe
N-kwe
N ___ ___ ___
Nkwe means leopard in Tswana

Tarentaal
Ta-ren-táál
T ___ ___ ___ ___ ___ ___ ___ ___
Tarentaal means guinea fowl in Afrikaans

Points To Ponder
The story is not all ~ let's explore some more!

1. When Noko was called back to the burrow by his parents, Noko dropped his furry little head and turned around to go back. How do you think Noko felt?

    a) happy

    b) angry

    c) disappointed

    d) sad

2. How would you feel if you heard that you were going to have a baby brother or sister?

3. What did Noko do to hurt his friend Inyoka in the forest?

4. Why did Noko do what he did to Inyoka?

5. Do you think Noko did this on purpose?

6. How could Noko have treated his friend Inyoka differently?

7. Do you think that when someone says hurtful things that it sticks to you like the quills stuck in Inyoka's scaly skin?

8. As a good friend, what can we do to prevent an angry friend's quills from shooting out at us or anyone else?

9. What did Noko do to show that he respects his friends when Mmabudu approached him?

10. Why is it so important to apologize to your friends if you had hurt them?

11. Why is it important that we forgive our friends if they hurt us is some way?

12. How would you feel if your friends did not forgive you when you accidentally hurt them?

13. Why do you think it was important for Mmabudu to step forward and address Noko's behavior toward Inyoka?

14. Which of the following are ingredients of a great friendship?

    a.   spending time together;

    b.   sharing ideas & treats;

    c.   caring for each other's safety & wellbeing;

    d.   respecting each other's differences;

    e.   all of the above

15. What can you do to be a better friend?

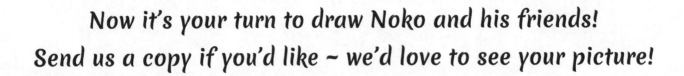

Now it's your turn to draw Noko and his friends!
Send us a copy if you'd like ~ we'd love to see your picture!

Please go to www.elenitheodorou.com to submit your picture by completing the online form.

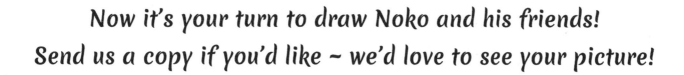

Now it's your turn to draw Noko and his friends!
Send us a copy if you'd like ~ we'd love to see your picture!

Please go to www.elenitheodorou.com to submit your picture by completing the online form.

Eleni Theodorou holds a bachelor's and honor's degree in psychology from the University of Pretoria in South Africa, and a master's degree in sports psychology from Capella University in the United States.

She has worked with children and their parents in different parts of Africa, the United Kingdom, and the United States, administering brain-based learning assessments and related coaching in pursuit of educating and empowering them academically, socially, and emotionally. Theodorou is also a dedicated volunteer to special needs children, young adults, and senior citizens.

Born and raised in South Africa, she currently lives in the United States, where she is an avid horse rider and enjoys Latin and ballroom dancing.

54512314R10029

Made in the USA
Charleston, SC
02 April 2016